ABOUT THE AUTHOR

Lee Bok

is not his real name.

If you bought this book thinking Lee Bok was his real name then you should be proud. You have passed the test and can turn the page. (You do that by holding the book in your left hand with the cover face up. With your other hand take one of your fingers and flick over a page, reading as you go.)

If you guessed that Lee Bok is a clever twist on a well-known brand then read on, as you will find contained within these pages many factoids of quite extraordinary inexactness.

CHAPTER 1

Chav History

Definitions of Chavs

- non-educated delinquents
- the burgeoning peasant
  underclass.

Chavs are identifiable by their attitude and clothes. Chavs want money and lots of it, but don't want to have to work for it.

Jodie Marsh and Jordan are obvious Chav icons. Reality shows, like *Big Brother*, and the Lottery are favourite TV programmes.

Chavs can be found far and wide, across the country, but go by different names depending on the location. In Scotland, on the West Coast, you'll find Neds (some say this is short for 'non-educated delinquents', others say it's short for Edward, as in teddy-boy). On the East Coast of Scotland they are known as Schemies (as in 'housing scheme').

Moving southwards to England, the range of names is staggering. In Liverpool they're called Scallies (as in loud, boisterous, disruptive or irresponsible people). Kev is quite common around London (probably because of the Harry Enfield inspired, idiotic teenage character Kevin). Then you have Janners (from Plymouth), Smicks, Spides, Moakes and Steeks (all from Belfast), plus

Bazzas, Pikeys (Essex), Charvers (Newcastle), Scuffheads, Stigs, Stangers, Yarcos, and Kappa Slappers (Kappa for girls who wear Kappa branded tracksuits, Slapper as in a promiscuous or crude female).

Although the general feeling is that the Chav name comes from the place of Chatham in Kent, it seems it has quite strong Gypsy connections. Chatham has had Gypsies living in it for generations. Interestingly, Chavi is the Romany word for child (and was recorded as far back as the 1850s), whereas Chavo means boy. By the late 1800s, Chavi was used to refer to an adult male. Another Gypsy connection is the word Charver (Romany for prostitute).

Pikey – also insulting – is more than likely to have come from the Kentish dialect term for Gypsy – a person who travels the roads.

CHAPTER 2

Chav Spotting

Chav Female / Chavette

According to the *Daily Mail*, the
females of the species *pull their
shoddily dyed hair back in that ultra-
tight bun known as a 'council-house*

facelift', wear skirts that would be better described as wide belts and tops that expose too much. It is true that stilettos are the favoured alternative footwear to trainers. Mark One and New Look outfits are always, and most definitely, in.

Hair tends to be bottle-blonde and scraped back into a ponytail, with lots of mousse and / or hairspray, scrunchies, etc.

Chav Male / Chavo

He wears an England shirt at least three times a week, spanking white trainers, trackie bottoms, and a hard, shifty expression. Attitude is everything, as is the latest cap (the cap logo changes on a regular basis).

A shaved head is good. Otherwise, hair stencilling is equally popular – with free styles as well as football team logos and favourite brands like Nike all the rage. Other favourites include slick partings, fringe flicks, curtains, and loads of hair gel.

Sorted!

CHAPTER 3

Famous Chav Role Models

Role Models

 Chris Moyles

 Christina Aguilera

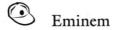 Danniella Westbrook

Eminem

Jade Goody

 Jessie Wallace

 Jodie Marsh

 Jordan

 Mel C

 Michelle (BB)

 Paris Hilton

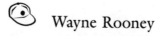 Peter Andre

 The Beckhams

 Wayne Rooney

CHAPTER 4

Chav Talk

Language

Expletives are helpful and used as frequently as possible, varying in crudeness depending on how much cider has been drunk or how much glue has been sniffed by said Chav.

"Fuck" punctuates sentences when vocabulary is elusive or just lacking. "Fucking" replaces adjectives and "cunt" replaces a person.

?*!*

Favourite sayings

"Bitch" (woman / girlfriend)

"Blazin" (very good)

"Bone" (erection)

"Brethern" (brothers and close
friends)

"Buzzin" (expression of approval)

"Check it" (look at it)

"Chuffed" (pleased with oneself)

"Coffin dodger" (old person)

"Cushty" (cool – a term first used
by Del Trotter!)

"Diss" (to disrespect)

"Dob on" (inform on someone –
to the police)

"Fit" (attractive)

"Floor it" (drive very fast)

"Givin it large" (overdoing things)

"Gov" (authority figure)

"Homeez" (friends)

"Innit" (Isn't it?)

"Knob jockey" (homosexual)

"Maccy D's" (MacDonald's)

"Minger" (a very ugly person)

"Not a prayer" (no chance)

"Preggers" (pregnant)

"Rat-arsed" (blind drunk)

"Solid" (referring to a strong /
reliable person)

"Spark up" (to light a fag)

"Steamin" (drunk as a skunk)

"Talent" (good-looking girl)

"Trek" (go on a long journey)

"Wheels" (a car)

"Wire it" (start a car without a key
or the owner's permission)

"Wot u fuckin say?" (Pardon?)

"Wot u lookin at?" or "Wot da fuck
you lookin at?" (Is something
the matter?)

Topics of conversation

Football, fighting, sex, *Big Brother*,
being bored, winning the Lottery,
Argos catalogues, the latest Nike
advert on the box, Kung Fu,
Coronation Street, *Bad Girls*,
Footballers' Wives, *Eastenders*, Trisha,
sex, money, becoming rich by doing

nothing, being spotted by the producer of a reality TV show and becoming famous, sex, money, being bored . . . zzzzzzzzzzzzzzzzzzzzzz zzzzzzzzzzzzzzzzzzzzzzzzzzzzzzzzz zzzzzzzzzzzzzzzzzzzzzzzzzzzzzzzzz zzzzzzzzzz.

CHAPTER 5

Chav Lifestyle

Jobs

Generally, Chavs spend most of their time unemployed but still manage to get hold of the latest trainers, have plenty of cigarettes and generally succeed in drinking to their hearts' content.

Chavs like money (especially when they haven't had to work for it) because spending it enables them to display STATUS.

If a Chav can get by on the dole, s/he will. There are, however, some typical jobs out there for the willing:

For Chavettes

Trainee hairdresser

Trainee beautician

Cleaner

Barmaid

For Chavos

Cowboy builder / plumber / roofer

Market stall trader

Mechanic

Security guard

For either

Checkout cashier at Lidl,
Netto or Aldi.

Fast food restaurant employee.

And at last but not least, the ultimate Chav summer job . . . Holiday rep – Spain, the Canary Islands, and of course Ibiza!

Attitude

The answer to everything is attitude.

Chavs are eye-contact aggressive. If anyone dares to look them in the eye it is assumed that they are asking for a fight or a kick up the backside.

?*!*

Only loners are picked on by Chavs,
though, because otherwise the Chav
pack (usually a group of about seven)
would have to leg it.

And this would not be cool.

Chavs have an inbuilt mechanism that encourages disrespect for all authority, whether it comes in the form of parents, a policeman, pub landlord or judge.

Shiftiness is the name of the game.

Books and Music

The *Sun*, *Daily Star* and the *Sport* (or the *Daily Mail* for the more cultured person) are about the only things Chavs even consider reading. And preferably someone else's copy.

Chav music consists mostly of Top 40 Rap (for the Chavos), R&B (for the Chavettes) and Dance (for both sexes). Favourites are Eminem, The Streets, anything Garage, Craig David, D12, 50 Cent.

Diet

Chav food and drink consists of
Supernoodles, Pot Noodles, weed,
beer, cheap cider, and MacDonald's
for Sunday lunch . . .

Hang-Outs

MacDonald's, KFC, Burger King, shopping centres, off licences, bus shelters, street corners...

To sum up, Chavs' leisure pursuits
are: spending all their dole money
on brand-named sports gear and
blinding, whiter-than-white trainers;
taking a decent car and turning it
into an ugly, noisy, street-racing
novelty; cadging cigarettes off
passers-by; smoking cheap cigarettes;

talking rubbish; starting a fight;
picking on loners; clubbing.

CHAPTER 6

Chav Clothes

Brands

The Burberry brand is reckoned
to be the number one brand but
other brands do come in and out of
fashion. A few years ago Polo and
Tommy Hilfiger were worn all over
the place but recently they have lost

their popularity with most Chavs.

At the moment the following brands are very popular (but remember that this list is not a definitive one as the scene is ever-changing!) . . .

In no particular order:

Hackett

Nickelson

Reebok

Nike

Tiffany

Louis Vuitton

Burberry

Von Dutch

Stone Island

Henry Lloyd

Aquascutum

Rockport

Although many Chavs bring back counterfeit clothes from the Costa, it is important in a Chav's existence to aspire to the genuine article. With a Burberry cap costing more than a week's job-seeking allowance, Chavs will pull out all the stops to get their gear.

Some of the gear in question is now so identified with Scallies in certain towns that shopping centres have banned the wearing of baseball caps altogether. One pub chain has even gone as far as to ban from their pubs anyone wearing some of the most prestigious brands in the country including Burberry and Aquascutum. This will come as a shock to the Prime Minister, Tony Blair, as he was spotted on holiday wearing a Burberry polo shirt. Even Victoria Beckham would be shown the door!

Sports gear
(although Chavs don't go near sports centres)

Again . . . brand, brand, and nothing but the brand!

White Nike trainers, tops and tracksuit bottoms with (preferably prominent) Burberry, Hackett, Nickelson, Reebok, etc. logos are compulsory. Don't forget – brands represent that all-important status. And sports gear is . . . well . . . cool.

Hats

A baseball cap – preferably in Burberry check – is a must-have accessory, put on at a very weird angle. Or a woolly Benny is good.

Trousers

Trackie bottoms tucked into football boots are much loved. Other favourites are Kappa button-ups, stonewashed jeans, special gold shells.

Footwear

'Prison white' Nike trainers are great for that permanently 'brand new' look. Red Adidas, or desert boots are good. White socks go without saying.

For the boys

England shirts – to be worn at
least three times a week; open
jackets (lest said England shirts'
logos be obscured); polo shirts;

sweatshirts; socks pulled
up over trackie bottoms;
collar turned up.

For the girls

Favourites are wide belts (aka mini skirts); cropped tops (to reveal not-overly-toned stomach); scrunchies; stilettos (an acceptable

alternative to trainers); Shoefayre,
BWise, Woolies, Poundstretcher,
Mark One items.

CHAPTER 7

Chav Jewellery

BLING! is the word.

Chavs love flashy, trashy jewellery and lots of it – heavy chains, big sovereign rings and chunky bangles, often bought from the jewellery counter at Argos or Index. Jacob watches are THE things for Chavs to wear. Costing in excess of £4,000, Chavs will do almost anything to get one. At a pinch, a good fake one will pass. Their large range of jewellery will impress anyone who has gone to Argos. Chunky gold chains costing up to a grand are the pinnacle of taste and status. The bigger, the better – this gives the wearer street cred and that is all-important in

Chavworld. For those with no local branch of Argos, help is at hand on the Freeview TV channel *Bid Up TV*. Watch this for a while and appreciate the great range of Chav jewellery.

CHAPTER 8

Chav Towns

This list has been put together with absolutely no care or attention whatsoever. The publishers take no responsibility for any person using this list of towns purely as a guide to find a Chav-free place to move to. If you do use this list in this way, then you deserve all that is coming to you!

The towns are in no particular order, but start with Chatham, alleged birthplace of the Chav phenomenon. This is amazing really – if you have ever been to Chatham, you'll no doubt agree.

A couple of years ago the *Observer* newspaper wrote a piece about Chatham and the Chavs that inhabit the town:

*Meet the Chatham girls, known as
'Chavs', whose fashion sense and
reputation for easy virtue have
earned them a global following as
worthy successors to their northern
neighbours. For years, Essex girls,
typified by actress Denise van Outen,
held the monopoly on short-skirted
peroxide-blonde stereotypes, prompting
questions in Parliament and essays
by Germaine Greer. But today the*

costume-jewellery crown has passed to their rivals from Chatham – young women, it is claimed, whose forbearers were kicked out of Essex 'for being too tarty'.

Chatham aside, other affected areas are

Atworth, Abingdon,

Littlehampton, Hamilton,

Portobello, Newcastle,

Greenock, Ambridge,

Anstruther, Ballamory,

Bar Hill, Barrow-in-Furness,

Basildon, Bath, Bedford,

Belfast, Bodmin, Bolton,

Farnham, Borchester,

Bournemouth, Dudley,
Brighton, Broxburn,
Cambridge, Carlisle, Catford,
Chester, Chichester, Coventry,
Cowdenbeath, Craigmiller,
Crawley, Livingston, Croydon,
Deal, Kettering, Derby, Dorking,
Liverpool, East Kilbride,
Eastleigh, Walford,

Eltham, Peterborough,

Londonderry, Plymouth,

Skegness, Weston-super-Mare,

Leeds, Swansea, Margate,

Sheffield, Weatherfield,

Glasgow, Grantham,

Cramond, Great Yarmouth,

Hackney, Hastings,

Scunthorpe, Headley Down,

Holby City, Holmefirth,
Emmerdale, Watford,
Streatham, Horsham, Kidlington,
Sutton Coldfield, Trowbridge,
Leicester, Leith, London,
Maidenhead, Middlesborough,
Immingham, Stoke-on-Trent,
Newport, Taunton, Cardiff,
Reading, Southampton, Newquay,
Sun Hill, Oxted, Wolverhampton,

Paisley, Las Vegas, Enfield,
Port Talbot, Hull, Rainham,
Ramsgate, Henley-on-Thames,
Redhill, Saffron Walden,
Portsmouth, Penrith, Folkestone,
Sunderland, Darlington,
Preston, Swindon, Thamesmead,
Lewisham, Winchester, Wrexham.

There are certain towns that are
more noteworthy than others.
Here are a few:

Hull

For most people, Hull is somewhere
to get a ferry from and not to hang

about in. However, knowing that John Prescott and Dan from *Big Brother* come from Hull might make you want to stop for a look round the next time you belt down the M62. If that is not enough incentive, try stopping off at Burger King or KFC on a Friday night. Hull has one of the highest teenage pregnancy rates in the UK. It is good fun to watch teenage mums sharing their chips with their one-month-old babies.

Taunton

The main shopping drag can be a bit patchy for Chav spotting in normal shopping hours. However with

Poundstretcher on the other side of the river, a brisk walk is all that is needed to spot Somerset's finest cider-swilling Chav specimens.

Chichester

This far south is an affluent area and home to the well-spoken Chav ("What youoo fuckin' looking at old boy?"). Having been ejected from their private schools because they were not up to A'levels, they have a certain posh charm but are just rich Chavs at the end of the day. The city centre pubs have theme nights – 'Pint and a Fight!' – on Fridays and Saturdays. With more money than sense, Chavs have renamed the town Shitchester. Bless!

Basildon

The capital of Essex Chavdom,
this is a place so full of Chavos
and Chavettes that non-Chavs will
definitely feel out of place here.
For the Basildon Chav, the centre
of the universe at the weekend is

the Festival Leisure Park. The local
council call this an 'entertainment
super centre' but, as anyone who
has been there on a Saturday night
will tell you, it is far from super!
Chavos and Chavettes from miles
around come here and hang around
outside as they are skint and cannot
go in. Many people have visited
this centre, seen the future of the
country and subsequently emigrated

post haste. This is really not for the faint hearted. Another place to avoid is the Wat Tyler Country Park. Wat Tyler – for those of you who are educated – was the geezer who started the Peasants' Revolt in 1300 something. He ended up getting killed by the King of that time. The park is now a centre of special scientific interest and a place where peasants can feel truly at home. Avoid!

So what started in the Kent area
of England has spread throughout
the United Kingdom and shows no
sign of stopping. It has even crept
abroad to Dublin and certain towns
in Spain. The Spanish connection
is probably down to Brits, their
children and the hoards of Chavs

heading for sun and cheap Sangria every summer.

It is now nearly impossible to go anywhere in the mainland UK and not see Chavs. There is a rumour that the North of Scotland and the Islands off it are Chav-free. This statement will no doubt elicit a flood of letters from readers saying that the Shetlands are just a hot bed of Chavs. As part of my research for this book, I went to Inverness and Tobermory and they seemed Chav-free. I visited all the likely looking hang-outs and not one Chav did I see. I got so desperate to find one that I chased what I thought at a distance was a Burberry-cap-wearing

Chav, only to find out it was
some old age pensioner wearing
a tartan tammy!

One of the favourite TV
programmes for Chavettes and their
young is *Ballamory*. This was filming
while I was in Tobermory. (Well I
thought it was worth mentioning,
but my editor says I should get
out more.)

As long as you are not in the North
of Scotland you can become quickly
acquainted with Chav spotting. It is
amazing how fast you can become
adept at knowing where to find
them. As long as you remember not
to make eye contact you
should be fine (except if it's pub
chucking out time). Remember:
do not try chatting up a Chav bird
as this will lead to a good kicking

(which in my opinion you deserve)!

So . . . the list you've seen here is not set in stone. If you have any towns to add, please send your suggestions to: chavs@crombiejardine.com.

CHAPTER 9

Chav Names

Spellings and pronunciations may vary, but here are some top names for Chavettes and Chavos.

Tip: 'T' is often silent, so 'Katie' is pronounced 'Kay-ee'; 'Th' is normally 'f', so 'Nathan' becomes 'Naffan' etc.

Chavettes

 Beckie

 Bianca

Britney

Casey

 Cassandra

 Caz

 Charmaine

 Chelsea

Stockport County

 Danielle

 Diamonique

 Donna

Jade

 Jemma

 Jordan

Syria

 Katie

 Kylie

 Leah

 Michelle

👜 Missy

👜 Monique

👜 Monneye

👜 Natalie

 Nikkie

 Rachelle (Shell)

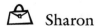 Samantha

 Sharon

👜 Shirley

👜 Stacie

👜 Tammy

👜 Tracie

Trish

Veronique

Vicky

Chavos

 Aaron

 Barry

Brandon

 Brooklyn

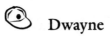 Corey

 Darren

 Dwayne

 Gary

Jason

Kevin

Lance

Larry

Lee

 Liam

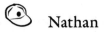 Nathan

 Rickie

Shane

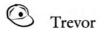 Trevor

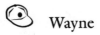 Wayne

Will

CHAPTER 10

Chav Updates
from Around the UK

If you have enjoyed reading this book and would like to know more about Chavs then there are some great sites on the web.

By far and away the best and most comprehensive Chav site is:

www.chavscum.co.uk

Other sites that are worth a look are:

www.youknowsit.co.uk

www.banburymassive.tk

www.glasgowsurvival.co.uk

www.scallycentral.com

www.hayezsquad.co.uk

www.stupidnorthernmonkey.co.uk

www.crombiejardine.com